Unnatural Symmetry

By Dermot Millar

About the Poet

Dermot Millar was born in Dublin Ireland in 1954 into a staunchly Catholic working-class family. He came to Canada with his parents and four siblings in 1966. Millar graduated from Simon Fraser University, with a B.A. in Criminology in 1979. For the next thirty-five years he worked in his field with distinction and raised a family. Throughout his life, Millar has been passionate about the act of writing, both as art and as a sacred place to share the joy and despair that joins all human life. In this collection of poems, Millar explores a range of subjects. From the vulnerability of early childhood to the anxieties of ageing, from politics to mental health, from sexuality to loneliness and from addiction to recovery. Millar's poetry illuminates with precision and truth in this post-modern alchemy of the written word.

To Sandra, my rock and true north star.

The Poems

1   Winter 1968

2   Suicide Subscriber

3   September Dawn

4   Snake Self

5   Digital Age

6   Confession 1963

7   For Mariam Ishag

8   Recovery

9   Back Yard Boot Heel Blues

10 Anxiety

11 Lone Wolf Pathology

12 In and Out

13 Chase

14 Scrotum Soul

15 Evenings Empire

Continued...

16	The Populist Outsider 2016
17	Unnatural Symmetry
18	Born and Raised
19	The Cherry Tree
20	Human Soap Bubbles
21	The Question
22	Progressive Insanities of an Older
23	Juggernaut
24	Alert the Neighbours
25	Saving the Moment
26	A Happy Poem for Mother
27	Death

Winter 1968

Empty skies
Low and grey
Flavor
Birch wood fires
And good hot tea
Holidays with Dickens
Or homespun tales
With brew

Suicide Subscriber

The night suicide showed its face
Looking for subscribers
Five plaid shirt weekend warrior men
Step in to one of their garages

Five beers to a round and everyone is drinking
Five souls all equipped to handle this intersection of testosterone
Each in their fleshy frame working hard to convince anyone
Of their adequacy

Stories differed but they all had the same feeling of want
Wanting validation from something outside themselves
Each thought themselves alone in their need

Meanwhile on the same street
Nine of the city's finest
Some with their guns drawn
Surround a man in his garage
Electrical cord wrapped
Tightly to a rafter at one end
And at the other end

His neck

Suicide is not illegal protested the man
Correct, agreed the finest
Our authority is to take you
To a psychiatric facility

And so they did

September Dawn

Grey dusty light slowly dissolves from blackness
The bulk of two lovers on opposing margins of the bed

Lovers once bound by a young passion that kissed the sky
Shattering the golden moon into a million silver stars

Lovers now bound by the joy of a shared life
And the scar of a thousand essential errands

Snake Self

Show the world your game face
None but the sages will see the Viper eat your eye ball
Arching your brain through your left eye socket
Kiss the babies and the grandmothers
Everyone loves your kisses and your game face

Some will sense the poison and think it is them
Exiting your brain through your right eyeball
Lean green Viper tail dangles from your left eye socket
Fate makes for strange meals and snake game faces

Digital Age

Life is rich but fast in the digital age
Into our souls' money and information does fly
With just one click we turn the page
Consume and consume until the day we die.

Click and click while we eat our food
All flavor and savor lost to speed
Off to therapy to improve our mood
Too fast we go for any advice to heed.

Before light came at the click of a switch
When walls had shadows not digital screens
Life was simpler but we were not so rich
So how to be rich and less harried human beings.

Listen to your heart beat and the pace of your breath
And digital speed will not cause your unnatural death.

Confession 1963

The confessional
Calls anonymously
Sins of commission and
Sins of omission heard
Mitigation by any measure irrelevant
Psychiatry not spoken
Victims not allowed
Priest's mirror and contrition
Required for dispensed penance and
Channeled blessing of God's absolution.

For Mariam Yahia Ibrahim Ishag

Shackled within her jail cell
Waiting for execution day
A toddler by her side
A baby on the way

Sentenced to death
For practicing her faith
Her children allowed to live
For its Mariam that they hate

A prisoner of conscience
Justice rendered by the unblind
There's no other explanation
For a sentence so unkind

Shackled in her jail cell
She is not forsaken or alone
For we are all Mariam
We all wait for the call home

Recovery

Omm...
Standing alone
Last layer of defense gone
Shame and all its circular relatives
Abated with forgiveness and self-love
Healing one mindful moment at a time
Omm...

Back Yard Boot Heel Blues

Basking in the glory of afternoon summer sun
When passes a banshee of fire engines roaring
To some sorry soul felled by a random event
Just like an insect under a boot heel

Anxiety

Between the mortal anchors
Of first and last breath
All sentients know anxiety
In blood, flesh and bone

Lone Wolf Pathology

Oh, Eat Me
That's how good I am
The world seems to disagree
Fuck the world
Where is my assault rifle?
I will show them
Who I am

.

In and Out

No invitation or consent
For entrance to the proceedings
Original sin washed away
Vulnerable always
No invitation or consent
At the end.

Chase

You know love and loneliness under the blazing sun
Something is missing but you know not what
Chase your passion into the insatiable hole
There you will not find what you are missing
However, you could live well in a relative universe
Full of other soap bubbles

Scrotum Soul

Vulnerable throat of arched cock
Jerked in wet pleasure with each spasm
Moist cargo launched into the holiest hour
Of evenings warm and fresh vagina

Oblivious to a future
Testosterone depleted scrotum soul
Limply awash in fantasy
Of his hard cock buggered juicy asshole

Evening's Empire

When evening's empire serves its last illusion
Swollen with satisfaction
I relish the notion I am God

Blasphemy shame shock
Broke hard a narcissistic rock

Humility

On the other hand
He did say he made us in his own image

The Populist Outsider 2016

It felt like brain damage
The physical state left by the toss and turn of an ordinary life
Little electric brain shocks firing like whiplash
Consciousness crashing in on itself
Cloves of garlic agitated in a skull shaped shelling bowl

The age of mass self-delusion is on us
The Alpha mingles with the Beta
The one with the predator eyes
They come and they go
With the ebb and the flow
Of passion for the object desired

Unnatural Symmetry

Sensitive poet soul pushed by fear of poverty shame
To live the compressed life of middle management bureaucrat
Who knows what comes out the other end of a life
Of such unnatural symmetry
How many are lost
In service to this existential choice.

The wisdom of follow your soul, passion, love
Your financial security will take care of itself
Is alien to thinking
An ideal for tomorrow more suited to retirement.

Reality is fear, anxiety, survival
A whirlwind of wolves at the door
Down the lane way, hiding in the bushes
Appearing in human form in public places
Disguises protected by the armour of social decorum
Do not confront them, or it is you that will be banished to the shame of poverty.

Born and Raised

Fear is his earliest
Most persistent companion.
Fear of everything.
The cold and unpredictable Irish weather.
The unpredictable people.

Father provided food and shelter.
He was a jeering master of terror.
In defense of his kids he beat people up.
His solution to every problem was kick them in the shins.
He thought drug dealers should be summarily shot.
He was known as "Billy the Bull" by many in his orbit.

Young Mother provided a home.
She was a master of extracting
Compliance from her five children.
An intimidator, a bully, and a shamer.
Mother was a master manipulator of love.
When these did not suit her violence
More out of control than was father's was her default.

The frock and flock of the Catholic church
A beehive of graceless self-interest.
Sisters of Mercy had no mercy.
Christian Brothers and Christian lay teachers
Assaulted their charges in more ways than three.

He could not contemplate a life without fear.
Life without fear was no more possible than life without breathing.
Fearful was who he was born and raised to be.

The Cherry Tree

Here I Sit.
Write something worthy.
Paralysis.
No, just write.
Let the words flow on to the page without edit.
And here I sit.
Waiting for god oh.
I pine for the pub of my childhood.
A pub on the corner
Of St. Peters Road
The Cherry Tree.

Human Soap Bubbles

His words a jungle of juxtaposition
Somehow arrived in consciousness
With the clarity of an expensive diamond

How should we live
How should we live well
How can we tell the difference
In a relative universe
Where soap bubbles
May be human.

The Question

You can't un-ring the bell
Or put the toothpaste back in the tube
But sooner or later all people hurt us
The question is whether
The relationship is worth the hurt.

Progressive Insanities of an Older

Stepping out of the shower
He noticed his penis sitting
Amongst his greying pubic hair
Looking like a dead mouse

In a fit of grief, he shaved the pubic hair
Now his penis looked like the head of a turtle
Neck dangling over a razor nicked
Inverted scrotum shell

He thought of firing squads
He thought of hunger
Of torture too
He remembered love
Awash in humility and gratitude
He prayed silently

Juggernaut

Consciousness is a juggernaut
Of razor peaks and dark valleys
From which I must find my bearing
Wobble Ouch Wobble Ouch Ouch ... I go

Shame and all its relatives
Arrive together for the gang bang
Of self-degradation underway

No conceivable distraction
Alone can help me
Unless I accept
Doing is the means
And the end

Alert the Neighbours

Rollicking stream of consciousness
Shows no leveling soon
Thoughts whole and fragmented
Cascading fast
Too fast to breathe.

There is no sense in any of it
Fear bubbles in orbit
Imminent calamity sensed
Phantom in-coming conjured
Nothing happens
Wrong again.

Screaming comes to mind
Don't want to alert the neighbours
Breathe.

Saving the Moment

I remember deleting my words in shame
Shame in myself
The full picture
Not just the pieces I want to be seen
Times when courage and integrity were present
Not the occasions when desperation had taken over
Or tiredness and loneliness so wearisome
No amount of courage and integrity
Could save the moment

A Happy Poem for Mother

A Lady Warrior of the highest ranks
She does for others without expecting thanks

The Heart of a lion fills her chest
She always tries her very best

With a hearty laugh and sense of fun
Her greater vintage is seldom won

From the fire of youth to wisdom's bend
She is my mother until the very end

Death

Death
Untimely, mysterious
Plundering, unforgiving, slaughter
Most common of destinations
Silence

Thanks for Reading!

Made in the USA
Columbia, SC
31 December 2017